BEAUTIFUL OWLS

PORTRAITS

of

ARRESTING
SPECIES

BEAUTIFUL OWLS

PORTRAITS

of

ARRESTING SPECIES

by MARIANNE TAYLOR
photographed by ANDREW PERRIS

Ivy Press

British Library Cataloguing in Publication Data
A catalogue record for this book is available from the British Library

This book was conceived, designed and produced by

Ivy Press
210 High Street, Lewes, East Sussex, BN7 2NS, UK

Creative Director Peter Bridgewater
Publisher Susan Kelly
Art Director Wayne Blades
Senior Editors Jayne Ansell & Jacqui Sayers
Designer Ginny Zeal
Photographer Andrew Perris
Illustrator David Anstey

ISBN: 978-1-908005-97-7
First Edition: 2013
Printed in China
Colour origination by Ivy Press Reprographics
Distributed worldwide (except North America) by Thames & Hudson Ltd.,
181A High Holborn, London WC1V 7QX, United Kingdom.
10 9 8 7 6 5 4 3 2 1

CONTENTS

Introduction 7

THE OWLS *20*

REPORTAGE *94*

Glossary *110*

Sanctuaries *110*

Charities *111*

Index *112*

INTRODUCTION

OWLS HAVE LONG HELD A SPECIAL PLACE IN OUR imaginations. They are perhaps the most recognizable of all birds, with their forward-facing, intensely expressive eyes giving them an almost human appearance. However, while we can all instantly identify the image of an owl, few of us have seen many of them in the wild, because owls lead mysterious lives. Most spend their active hours in the double darkness of deep forest at nighttime, and if it weren't for their haunting cries we might never know they were there.

With their mysterious, almost spooky ways, it is little wonder that owls are associated with magic and menace in a range of cultures around the world. In folk tales, they are the familiars of witches, their appearance foretells death and disaster, and they have wisdom beyond all other creatures. These ideas have certainly influenced the way that people have treated owls over the years, sometimes with reverence and sometimes with total intolerance – in some cultures the killing of owls is much encouraged.

The reality of owl life is no less intriguing. They are

Above: Owl sanctuaries give a unique opportunity to get a close view of these beautiful, enigmatic birds.

perfectly adapted to hunt their prey in near darkness. Their plumage often bears gorgeously complex and intricate patterning, allowing them to blend in with the bark and branches of trees as they sleep through the daylight hours. Many owls forge lifelong partnerships with their mates – affirmed with hours of tender closeness, sharing a branch and affectionately preening each other's plumage. However, when the territory needs to be defended, they become a devastating attack force, capable of driving off all challengers.

Owls may not be quite as all-knowing as legend would have us believe, but they are intelligent birds, and have long been popular with falconers and bird keepers as they are usually easy to train and often very affectionate. Sanctuaries for owls, whether for wild birds that needed to be rescued, or birds born and raised in captivity, allow us to observe them at close quarters and truly appreciate their extraordinary beauty. This book features stunning photographs taken at such sanctuaries, which will introduce you to some of the most beautiful and enigmatic birds in the world.

OWLS IN CIVILIZATION

THE HUMAN FASCINATION WITH OWLS CAN BE traced back to the earliest civilizations. The hieroglyphs of Ancient Egypt used a representation of an owl for the letter 'm'. Among the 30,000-year-old cave paintings in Chauvet Cave, France, is an image of an owl turning its head 180 degrees to look behind itself – one of the many uncanny owl talents that have long inspired both admiration and suspicion.

The Ancient Greeks held owls in high regard. As the chosen birds of the goddess of wisdom, Athene, owls were protected from harm and nested in profusion around the Acropolis in Athens. The supposed wisdom of the owl was inspired both by its expressive face and its ability to see at night – as if it had a magical ability to cast its own light into the darkness. As owls were seen as protectors, because of their vigil-like wakefulness at night, armies carried images of them into battle and took owl sightings as a sign of sure victory.

However, in ancient Roman culture, owls had very different associations and the sight or sound of an owl was considered to foretell a death. Several notable deaths, including that of Julius Caesar, were said to have been predicted by an owl.

In England in the Middle Ages, people from all tiers of society practised falconry. As owls are primarily nocturnal, they have obvious limitations as falconry birds, but tethered owls were used to attract wild hawks, which the falconers would catch. Modern falconers do train and fly owls, especially the larger eagle owl species.

Superstitions surrounding owls are still prevalent in some cultures. In parts of Africa, witchdoctors use owl body parts when creating spells. In Madagascar, owls are widely considered to be extremely unlucky, to the extent that when an owl is found it is often killed simply because the finder is afraid of it.

In general, however, owls are popular and much loved. They appear with increasing frequency in children's books and films, and owl-themed jewellery and fashion is more popular than ever. As birdwatchers learn more about wild birds, and owl sanctuaries provide opportunities to get close to tame owls, the mystique of the owl is evaporating but its magic remains as compelling as ever.

Above: An owl hieroglyph detail from Luxor (Thebes), Egypt. In some cultures owls bore the role of supernatural protector.

EVOLUTION OF OWLS

OWLS, LIKE ALL BIRDS, ARE THOUGHT TO DESCEND from the theropod dinosaurs. These were a group of mainly predatory dinosaurs, some big and some small, that had feathers (but did not fly) and ran on two well-developed hind legs – *Tyrannosaurus rex* is a familiar example. The earliest fossils we have that are classed as birds rather than feathered dinosaurs date back about 225 million years, but recognizable fossil owls didn't appear until much more recently – between 55 and 65 million years ago.

By studying the DNA of birds that are alive today, it is sometimes possible to work out how much shared evolutionary history different bird groups have. For example, owls, in an evolutionary sense, are closely related to the diurnal birds of prey or raptors, such as hawks, eagles, falcons and their relatives, and, more surprisingly, to parrots. But paradoxically, the bird group they share the most obvious similarities with are the nightjars, which are nocturnal birds with intricate plumage patterns, silent flight and far-carrying voices. But they are not closely related in an evolutionary sense; it

Above: The Galapagos Short-eared Owl has evolved darker colouring than its mainland cousins, providing camouflage on the lava rocks.

appears they evolved similar traits merely because they have a similar way of life.

When the owl lineage first separated from those of other bird groups, these early owls were probably very different to the owls we know today, and also much more diverse; some became heron-like, others more like ground-living hawks. However, only the owls that took to the trees have survived to the present day. At first, the barn owl group dominated, but over time, as environments have changed, other owl types have become more numerous – a situation which continues today.

Some of the most interesting examples of owl evolution can be seen on small islands. Owls that colonize islands tend to become adapted in special ways that make them distinct from their cousins on the mainland. For example, the subspecies of SHORT-EARED OWL that lives on the Galapagos Islands has learned to hunt a type of small seabird known as a storm petrel by lying in wait for them when they return to their nests at dusk. In Indonesia, many tiny islands have their own unique species of scops owl.

OWL SPECIES

THE OWLS LIVING TODAY CAN BE DIVIDED INTO two main groups or families. The family Tytonidae contains about 26 species of barn owls and bay owls, while the remaining 224 or so species are in the family Strigidae, or 'true owls'.

The barn owl group is distinctive in several ways. Most species are pale-coloured, with whites, golden tones and greys predominant in their plumage, rather than brown shades. They have long legs and long faces, which are more heart-shaped than rounded. They have very dark eyes and lack ear tufts. Many barn owls are birds of open countryside, while the bay owls live in thick forest.

The large family Strigidae contains all other owls, and there is a great deal of diversity within this family, with several distinct groupings. The wood owls form the genus *Strix*. They are medium to large, with big, un-tufted heads, and are nocturnal woodland birds with hooting calls and beautiful, patterned plumage. Examples include the TAWNY OWL of Europe, the BARRED OWL of North America and the GREAT GREY OWL, found across the northern hemisphere.

Above: Ear-tufts may be used for camouflage and possibly also for non-vocal communication between pairs and young families.

The largest of all owl are the eagle owls, which make up the genus *Bubo*. These are very powerful birds, often at the top of the food chain. Most have obvious ear tufts. In Europe, they are represented by the EUROPEAN EAGLE OWL and in North America by the GREAT HORNED OWL.

The scops owls form another very large group. These also have ear tufts but are small or very small, mainly eat insects and have whistling voices. They are found in Europe, Asia and Africa, but are very closely related to the screech owls of America.

The hawk owls of Asia and Australasia are rather unusual, having long tails, quite pointed faces and bulging, startled-looking eyes. The BOOBOOK, Australia's best-known owl, belongs to this group. Among the smallest species of owls are the pygmy owls, which are forest birds found in most parts of the world. Although tiny, they are fierce and powerful hunters.

Although many owls have ear-tufts, the name 'eared owls' refers to a distinct group of species that belong to the genus *Asio*. These are all slim, shy owls that choose to live in open countryside.

HUNTING, FEEDING & DIGESTION

ALL OWLS ARE HUNTERS OF LIVING PREY, AND THE larger species are among the most formidable predators on earth. The EUROPEAN EAGLE OWL, for example, can kill young deer and foxes, and birds of almost any size. At the other end of the scale, the LITTLE OWL feeds mainly on insects.

Most owls hunt by night, so possess various adaptations to help them find their prey in the darkness (see page 12). Quite a few species are crepuscular (most active at dawn and dusk), but only a few are truly diurnal.

When hunting in flight, owls fly low and slowly, heading into the wind and using it for lift. BARN OWLS fly back and forth over patches of long grass, listening for voles moving below. This flight is energetic, with much vigorous flapping and hovering. Without some wind, an owl would expend too much energy for this kind of hunting style to be worthwhile, so on very still or very windy nights it will switch to static hunting from a perch.

Little Owls and many other species also hunt from perches, and when they see or hear movement they quickly drop down and pounce on

Above: The owl's hunting strategy is low and slow, and its superb hearing helps it detect the faintest rustle below.

the prey. If the first attack misses, the owl may chase after its prey on foot. The fish owls, including the huge BLAKISTON'S FISH OWL, wade into shallow water to find fish. GREAT GREY OWLS and other wood owls can punch their feet through several centimetres of laying snow to grab prey they hear moving underneath. TAWNY OWLS sometimes target roosting birds, flying along hedges at dusk and trying to scare the birds into taking flight where they can easily be caught.

Owls usually seize their prey with one or both feet, and kill it with a powerful squeeze of the talons and sometimes a bite. The owl will then usually carry the prey away to a safe, secluded spot to eat it, as the commotion of the hunt may attract other predators that would attempt to steal the prey.

Owls' digestive tracts are adapted to allow them to swallow their prey whole, although large prey is eaten in pieces. The swallowed prey is 'processed' in the owl's gizzard, a muscular part of the stomach, and indigestible parts proceed no further. Instead, they are compacted into a pellet, which the owl later regurgitates.

SENSES

AS A GROUP, BIRDS SHOW MUCH LESS VARIETY IN their general anatomy than do some other animal groups – mammals, for example. However, some of the most striking anatomical adaptations of any birds are seen in the nocturnal owls, and in particular in their senses.

Owls have very large eyes, and so are able to gather plenty of light, but because the eyeball is tube-shaped rather than spherical, it is less bulky than a similarly powerful round eyeball. The payoff is that owls have a narrower field of vision and also cannot move their eyes side to side as they are fixed in bony sockets. Owls compensate for this lack of eye movement by having very flexible necks so they can move their heads very freely – an owl can turn its head almost 360 degrees.

Another eye adaptation is the 'tapetum lucidum' – a fine sheet of reflective tissue behind the owl retina. Light entering the eye reaches the retina where it is absorbed by light-gathering cells, but any that passes through is reflected back by this special adaptation, giving a second chance for it to be absorbed.

Above: Owls have acute hearing and vision, making them highly successful hunters. Their large eyes are almost fixed in their sockets.

For many owls, hearing is even more important than vision. Owl ear openings are on the sides of the head, and some owls have the two ears set at different heights, meaning that they can also accurately judge the distance of sounds that are coming from directly above or below by comparing which ear hears the sound first. With this ability to pinpoint a sound in three-dimensional space, an owl can target and catch a mouse moving under fallen leaves without needing to see it at all. The sense of touch is also important here – sensitive filoplume feathers on the feet help the owl feel exactly where the prey is. Owls also have these filoplumes on their faces, and they are helpful when dealing with prey held in the talons, as their eyes cannot focus on objects that are very close.

Besides hearing, animal ears also contain the vestibular system, which helps to give them a sense of balance. In owls this is highly developed and allows them to hold their heads level and steady when their bodies are tilting and turning in active flight. The ear canals contain tiny otoliths or 'ear rocks', whose movement as the owl turns its head is fed back to the brain.

EYES & EARS

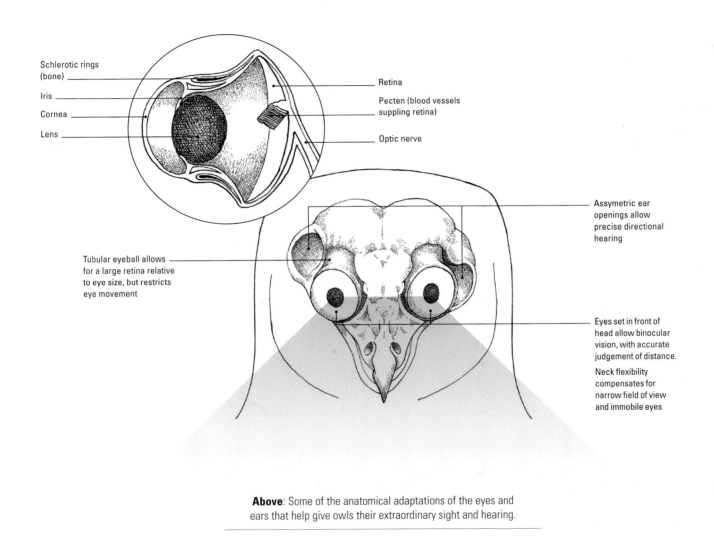

Schlerotic rings (bone)

Iris

Cornea

Lens

Retina

Pecten (blood vessels suppling retina)

Optic nerve

Tubular eyeball allows for a large retina relative to eye size, but restricts eye movement

Assymetric ear openings allow precise directional hearing

Eyes set in front of head allow binocular vision, with accurate judgement of distance.

Neck flexibility compensates for narrow field of view and immobile eyes

Above: Some of the anatomical adaptations of the eyes and ears that help give owls their extraordinary sight and hearing.

FEATHERS & FLIGHT

A BIRD'S FEATHERS SERVE SEVERAL FUNCTIONS. They provide warmth, with a soft, fluffy layer of down to hold warm air, and a smooth, waterproof outer 'shell' to keep heat in. They form a canvas for camouflaged or decorative colours and patterns. Perhaps most importantly, they allow the bird to fly.

In general, owls have very thick and dense plumage, giving them their round shape, disguising their often quite long necks and legs, and making them look a lot larger than their body weight would suggest. Owls native to cold climates have the thickest plumage, which often extends to a thick feather covering on the legs and toes, parts of which are bare and scaly in most birds.

The colours in owl plumage are the result of two pigments – eumelanin, which gives black, grey and dark brown tones, and phaeomelanin, which gives reds and lighter browns. With just these two pigments on their feathers, owls' plumage shows a wonderful variety of intricate and complex patterning, primarily to camouflage the bird and help it stay as invisible as possible when it is asleep during the daytime.

Many owls have two pointed tufts on their heads, one on either side. These are called 'ear tufts' as their shape and position resemble the pointed ears of a cat, but they have no relation to the actual ears of the owl. Their function is thought to be one of camouflage, giving the owl silhouette an angular shape that is more like a broken branch than a living creature. It is also thought that they may be used for communication.

Owls' wings are generally rather short and broad, although the barn owls have proportionately longer and slimmer wings. Short, wide wings are not good for speed but do provide manoeuvrability, which is useful for birds whose flight paths go through dense woodlands with many obstacles along the way.

The owl flight feather shows some notable adaptations that help minimize sound from the bird's wing beats. The upper surface of the feather is soft and velvety, and along its leading edge there is a comb-like structure, which helps break up the airflow. This means that when an owl is in flight, there is no whooshing of wing against air that would alert its prey to its presence.

Above: While wings provide the power for flight, the tail helps with steering and braking.

BASIC ANANTOMY

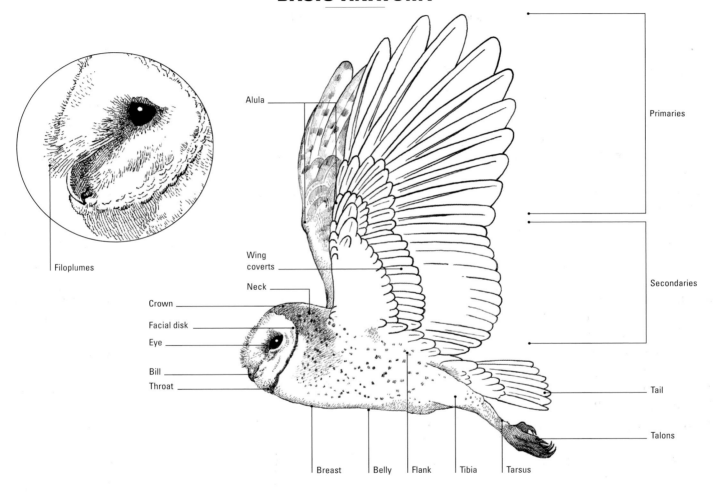

Filoplumes

Alula

Wing coverts

Neck

Crown

Facial disk

Eye

Bill

Throat

Breast

Belly

Flank

Tibia

Tarsus

Primaries

Secondaries

Tail

Talons

Above: The basic anatomy of an owl, showing different types of feathers and other features.

CALLS & BREEDING

BEING ACTIVE AT NIGHT, OWLS COMMUNICATE mostly by sound. Most of the calls they make are associated with breeding behaviour, and calls and songs are an important part of their courtship rituals.

Male owls have a territorial song, which they may give for hours on end early in the breeding season. It usually consists of a set series of notes, which may be booming hoots, shrill whistles, or somewhere in between – the bigger the owl, the deeper its voice. This song has two purposes – to discourage rival males from challenging for the territory, and to attract females. Once the male owl has a mate, she will join in with his song, usually with a very similar song of her own. This 'duetting' tells other owls around – males and females – that the territory is occupied. The bonded pair also 'converse' together with other, quieter calls.

Most owls are monoga-mous for the duration of the breeding season at least, and many pair for life, staying together all year round, and using the same nesting site year after year. Good nest sites are hard to find and owls show great loyalty to them. Most species nest in holes in

Above: In the nest, owlets compete with their siblings to get enough food from their parents.

trees – the smaller owls will often use holes made in previous years by nesting woodpeckers. Larger owls may nest on crags, in old stick nests built by other birds, or on the ground.

Some owls lay only two eggs, while others may lay 10 or more. The female usually lays eggs every other day, but begins to incubate as soon as the first egg is laid. This means the first egg will hatch before the second, and so on. Because the chicks are of different ages and sizes, the oldest and strongest will always be fed first. And because of this, the youngest chicks will quickly starve if there is a shortage of food. It may seem brutal, but this strategy prevents the whole brood from perishing.

Chicks often leave the nest before they can fly, and live in nearby branches. The parents continue to bring food for several weeks. After this, the real challenge begins, as the young owls must leave their parents' territory and find hunting grounds of their own. The first winter is a very testing time for a young owl, and mortality is high. If they make it to the next spring, though, they have a good chance of living a long life.

HABITAT & MIGRATION

WE THINK OF OWLS AS WOODLAND BIRDS, AND most species do stick to woods or forests, but almost every other habitat type in the world has at least one species of owl associated with it. Of course, there are many different kinds of woodland too, and all have their own kinds of owls.

Many owls, including the NORTHERN HAWK OWL and GREAT GREY OWL, live in the northern pine forests near or within the Arctic Circle. Their dense, warm plumage protects them from the cold, and they are strong enough flyers to fly south to warmer places in severe winters. In the treeless tundra further north, the SNOWY OWL's thick white plumage provides warmth and camouflage in an often snowy landscape.

In warmer climates, many owls live in woodland and specialize in establishing a very stable territory, which they come to know intimately. They learn the best spots to find prey and can hunt effectively on the darkest nights.

Open countryside offers good hunting opportunities for owls, and many species, such as the LONG-EARED OWL, choose habitats that include some woodland (with large

trees for nesting) and open areas for hunting. Other owls can do without trees, instead nesting on the ground. The SHORT-EARED OWL, for example, is adapted to live in truly open environments such as moorlands.

In the desert states of the US, large cacti make a good substitute for trees for nesting ELF OWLS. Another desert owl is the BURROWING OWL, which uses tunnels dug by animals such as prairie dogs for its nest sites. Some owls, such as the COMMON SCOPS OWL, have adapted to live in towns and sometimes hunt the swarms of insects that are attracted to street lights.

Most owls do not migrate, but some northern species do. Snowy Owls, for example, may move thousands of kilometres south in harsh winters. Short-eared Owls, on the other hand, are nomadic, roaming widely and breeding wherever they find a good supply of food. Young owls of many species may have to wander hundreds of kilometres to find their own territory once they are independent of their parents. By contrast, most young TAWNY OWLS do not wander far, and will settle permanently just 4 km (2.5 miles) from their birthplace.

Above: Owls live in a range of habitats including woods, forests, farmland, savannahs, snow-covered open tundra, deserts and towns.

CONSERVATION

OUR WORLD IS CHANGING. FOR WILD ANIMALS, some of these changes are happening too quickly for them to adapt, and many species are declining severely. For others, change has created new opportunities that they can exploit. Among owls, there are winners and losers, and some, which have reached the brink of extinction, are now fighting back thanks to help from conservationists.

Habitat loss is the most serious threat to owls. Deforestation destroys suitable habitat, and many owls depend on large, mature trees for nesting. Even with tree-planting schemes, it can take decades or centuries for such habitats be restored. One way to help owls in this situation is to provide purpose-built nestboxes. This helped change the fortunes of the very rare BLAKISTON'S FISH OWL in Japan.

Excessive use of pesticides on farmland threatens owls, and is one of the causes of a severe decline in the BARN OWL in Britain during the 20th century. The owls may be poisoned by eating prey that has ingested the pesticide, or they may simply be unable to find enough prey to survive. Insect-eating owls, such as the COMMON SCOPS OWL, can be particularly badly affected.

In some countries, deliberate killing of owls, often for religious or superstitious reasons, can be a serious problem. Owls may also be killed because of their possible impact on game birds. Although all owls are protected in Britain, there are still cases every year of owls being illegally shot or trapped by gamekeepers.

In North America, the SPOTTED OWL is threatened both by habitat loss, and by competition with the BARRED OWL. Deforestation has enabled Barred Owls, which prefer lighter woodland, to encroach into Spotted Owl habitats, where they displace the Spotted Owls or, sometimes, hybridize with them.

About 75 owl species are considered to be at serious risk of extinction. These include the Spotted Owl, the SIAU SCOPS OWL of Indonesia, and the FOREST OWLET of India. Studying their behaviour will help conservationists find ways to protect them. Breeding in captivity, with a view to returning the young birds to the wild, can also help to save a species from extinction.

Above: Many species are currently under threat. Research and breeding programmes are underway to counteract this sad decline in numbers.

THE OWLS

Owls are *powerful, predatory* and *unpredictable* and yet with their dark, penetrating gaze, circular, human-like faces and cryptic plumage patterns, they continue to capture our hearts. Who could fail to fall for the fascinations of these *feathered phenomena?* Owls were an enigma...until now. Let's LIFT THE LID a little on these shy birds.

EURASIAN EAGLE OWL
BUBO BUBO

A truly magnificent bird, the EURASIAN EAGLE OWL is one of the world's largest and most powerful birds of prey, and is a fearsome predator. Eurasian Eagle Owls are popular with falconers, but must be handled with great care. In parts of their range, these owls have begun to nest in town centres, allowing many people to enjoy watching them at close quarters.

Features

There are many subspecies of Eurasian Eagle Owl, which vary in size and plumage colour. However, in all its forms this is a very large, solid and bulky owl, with a proportionately small head, and short wings and tail. The plumage is intricately patterned in shades of brown and grey, with vertical streaks on the chest and horizontal barring on the wings. It has an imposing expression, with deep orange eyes, and long, pointed ear tufts.

Hunting

Almost every bird and mammal that shares its habitat is on the menu – this owl can even kill young deer and fully grown foxes. When hunting, the owl usually looks out from a raised perch, before flying low and fast towards its victim.

Call & Song

The male's deep, hooting song has two notes, the first stronger than the second. This inspired the onomatopoeic scientific name *Bubo*. The female replies with a higher-pitched double hoot.

Size

Male ....58–70 cm (22¾–27½ in)

Female ....65–75 cm (25½–29½ in)

Wingspan ....150–188 cm (59–74 in)

Habitat & Distribution

This is an owl of patchy, open forests, rocky ground and, in some countries, suburban areas. Eurasian Eagle Owls are found across Europe and Asia, in a broad band from southern Spain to northern Japan.

WESTERN SIBERIAN EAGLE OWL
BUBO BUBO SIBIRICUS

The Eurasian Eagle Owl is a widespread species found across much of northern Asia. Like many widespread owls, it has several subspecies, including the WESTERN SIBERIAN EAGLE OWL. This owl is very large and very pale, and its creamy plumage and bright eyes make it strikingly beautiful. Like other eagle owls, it is a formidable predator of mammals and other birds.

Features

This owl is one of the larger subspecies of the Eurasian Eagle Owl, which makes it a huge bird. The plumage is light sandy brown on the upper side, and paler (almost white) on the breast and belly, giving the owl an almost ghostly appearance. The back and wing feathers are barred with darker grey, and the underside has fine, dark streaking. The eyes are orange-yellow, and the feet are covered in soft, cream-coloured feathers.

Hunting

Like other Eurasian Eagle Owls, this bird is a fearsome hunter and is the 'top predator' in its habitat, along with the lynx. It can kill any other bird of prey, even eagles, but its usual diet is medium-sized birds and mammals.

Call & Song

Territorial males and females give a deep, two-note hooting song. If agitated, this owl gives a stuttered series of rapid hoots. If startled from its roost, it flies off with a loud, croaky squawk.

Size

Male .... 65–72 cm (25½–28¼ in)

Female .... 70–75 cm (27½–29½ in)

Wingspan .... 165–188 cm (65–74 in)

Habitat & Distribution

This species lives in Arctic pine forest. Its range goes across Siberia, as far east as the Altai mountains and north to the edge of the tree line.

VERREAUX'S EAGLE OWL
BUBO LACTEUS

Sometimes known as the 'Milky Eagle Owl' because of the pale milky tones of its plumage, VERREAUX'S EAGLE OWL is the largest owl species found in Africa. This handsome owl is notable for its far-carrying call and unusual bright pink eyelids. In some areas, this owl lives on the edges of towns or quite close to people and can become fairly tame.

Features

Rather a slim, tall eagle owl, this bird is mainly soft light grey in colour, with fine, delicate darker barring. The facial disc is defined with thick, heavy, black lines, and the ear tufts are rather broad and blunt. This owl has very dark brown eyes, and the pink upper eyelids are visible even when the eyes are open wide, making the bird look rather sleepy.

Hunting

Verreaux's Eagle Owl is a versatile hunter, eating all kinds of prey from mammals and birds to reptiles, fish and moths. Like the other eagle owls, it usually sits on a favourite perch and swoops onto prey, but it also catches insects in flight and wades to catch fish.

Call & Song

Both sexes have a song with several regularly spaced grunting hoots, which carry over a long distance. The female also whistles when begging for food from her mate.

Size

Male .... 60–63 cm (23½–24¾ in)

Female .... 62–65 cm (24½–25½ in)

Wingspan .... 140–164 cm (55–64½ in)

Habitat & Distribution

This owl lives in the savannahs, thorny scrubland and light woodland of Africa south of the Sahara and is very widespread. It is endangered in areas where agricultural pesticides are used as it has difficulty finding enough prey.

SNOWY OWL

BUBO SCANDIACUS

The SNOWY OWL is unmistakable with its white plumage, which camouflages it against snow in its Arctic habitat. Although it lacks ear tufts, it is part of the eagle owl group and shares their large size and powerful build. It is a very well-known species, not least because the most notable owl in the *Harry Potter* books and films is a Snowy Owl – Harry's own owl, Hedwig.

Features

This is a large and chunky owl with a round body, short tail and proportionately small head. Adult male Snowy Owls are almost completely white, while females and young birds have varying amounts of black speckling. The legs and toes are fully and thickly feathered. The eyes are bright yellow and often narrowed.

Hunting

Snowy Owls are mainly active by day, probably because they can't safely roost at this time – in their very open habitat they would be in full view of predators. They look out for prey from a rock or other raised perch then attack with a fast, low glide. The species eats mainly lemmings but also takes other mammals and birds.

Call & Song

Males sing with a series of booming, barking hoots. The female has a similar but higher-pitched song. Other, non-territorial calls include chirps and shrieks.

Size

Male	53–65 cm (20¾–25½ in)
Female	59–66 cm (23¼–26 in)
Wingspan	142–166 cm (56–65¼ in)

Habitat & Distribution

The Snowy Owl breeds across the whole Arctic region, north of the tree line, and migrates south in winter. The owl breeds on open tundra, so could suffer a serious decline in the future as a result of climate change.

INDIAN EAGLE OWL
BUBO BENGALENSIS

A beautiful, large owl with very long, upright ear tufts, the INDIAN EAGLE OWL is a fairly common bird of open countryside, well known to the people of the Indian subcontinent. This owl is a very popular species among falconers – they have been known to escape their handlers and set up home in towns, posing a danger to local cats and small dogs.

Features

This stocky owl has light brown plumage heavily marked with blackish-brown streaks (on the breast and belly) and mottling (on the back and wings). The facial disc is boldly outlined with black, and the long, quite slender ear tufts are mostly black. The owl has large, wide-spaced orange eyes with a stern expression, and feathered legs and toes.

Hunting

The diet consists mainly of small- to medium-sized mammals such as rats, and also birds and other vertebrates. Although this owl usually hunts by watching from a perch, it will also search for prey in flight, patrolling slowly at a low level. When the flying owl spots prey, it swings its feet forwards to grab it.

Call & Song

The Indian Eagle Owl's song is a two-note hoot, the second note stronger. If upset, the owl makes an angry hiss.

Size

Male ....50–53 cm (19¾–20¾ in)

Female ....52–56 cm (20½–22 in)

Wingspan ....130–145 cm (51¼–57 in)

Habitat & Distribution

This owl lives in India and some neighbouring countries (though not Sri Lanka – like many owls it is reluctant to make sea crossings). It prefers rugged, rocky landscapes, but it also lives in woodland and on town edges.

SPOTTED EAGLE OWL

BUBO AFRICANUS

The Spotted Eagle Owl is one of the smaller species of eagle owl. It is quite common in southern Africa, although it is often hunted because of superstitious beliefs. One female Spotted Eagle Owl became an internet celebrity due to her choice of nesting site – a large pot plant on a Johannesburg balcony. Her daily life was broadcast via a webcam aimed on the nest.

Features

This is a thickset owl with rather long wings. The main colour in its plumage is a soft grey, with fine, darker barring on its underside and darker and lighter speckles on the back and wings. The facial disc has a fine, dark border. With its triangular ear tufts and bright yellow eyes, it has a very cat-like look.

Hunting

Although this is a relatively big owl, its diet is dominated by insects, spiders and other invertebrates. However, the owl will also prey on larger animals, like lizards, frogs, rodents and small birds. Much of its hunting is from a perch, swooping down when it spots a potential meal, but it will also chase flying insects.

Call & Song

Male Spotted Eagle Owls have a song consisting of three short, quick hoots followed by a longer single hoot. Females join in with a similar song, the duet sounding as though it comes from just one bird.

Size

Male ....40–43 cm (15¾–17 in)

Female ....42–45 cm (16½–17¾ in)

Wingspan .....100–113 cm (39½–44½ in)

Habitat & Distribution

There are two separate populations of this owl – in southern Africa, and on the southern Arabian peninsula. It lives in light woodland, including suburban areas.

AMERICAN BARN OWL
TYTO FURCATA

Found almost everywhere in the USA and South America, the AMERICAN BARN OWL is very similar to the Barn Owl of Europe. This owl shows considerable variation across its wide range, with northern birds being much larger and paler than those of the South American forests.

Features

Across its wide geographic range, this sleek, leggy owl varies considerably, but most subspecies have a gingery-brown upper side with patches of grey, and a pale breast and belly with a scattering of fine, dark spots. The heart-shaped face is usually white and the rather small eyes are black. Females are darker and spottier than males. As with other barn owls, it has asymmetrically set ear openings.

Hunting

This owl hunts at night and searches for its prey from a perch. Sometimes it also hunts in flight, flapping slowly along close to the ground and hovering when it finds something. The pounce is a vertical drop, feet first. It eats mainly small mammals, but also sometimes birds and reptiles.

Call & Song

The call is a rather blood-curdling scream, which it gives both when flying and when perched. This serves as a territorial 'song'.

Size

Male	34–37 cm (13½–14½ in)
Female	35–38 cm (13¾–15 in)
Wingspan	90–100 cm (35½–39½ in)

Habitat & Distribution

American Barn Owls are found from southern Canada down to the tip of South America, including the Caribbean, and the Galapagos and Falkland Islands. Most of the subspecies live in open, grassy countryside, but some live in dense rainforest.

MOTTLED OWL

STRIX VIRGATA

Rather little is known about the Mottled Owl, a medium-sized wood owl from South America. This attractive owl is a shy bird that lives in various kinds of forests, active at night and spending its days asleep in hiding places deep within the forest foliage. Although the Mottled Owl is rarely seen, it can be heard on moonlit nights giving its hooting song.

Features

This owl has a rotund, round-headed shape. There are lighter and darker colour morphs, and also some variation between the four subspecies. The plumage is mottled grey-brown on the back and wings, and paler on the underside, with darker streaks and a strong, bright chestnut flush on the breast. The owl has large, dark brown eyes, outlined on their inner edge with pale feathers that contrast with the rest of its darker brown face.

Hunting

Mottled Owls are active at night only, when they hunt from a perch, using their acute hearing to detect small mammals on the ground or in trees. Their diet also includes small birds and insects, which may be caught in flight.

Call & Song

The territorial song of the male is a rather croaking hoot. The female's reply is similar but higher-pitched, and she also gives a more drawn-out, wailing note.

Size

Male	30–35 cm (11¾–13¾ in)
Female	32–38 cm (12½–15 in)
Wingspan	not known

Habitat & Distribution

The Mottled Owl is a woodland bird, commonest in lowland rainforests. Its range extends from Venezuela and Colombia down through most of Brazil and into northern Argentina. Deforestation is a threat to this species, and its numbers are declining.

ASHY-FACED OWL

TYTO GLAUCOPS

The Ashy-Faced Owl is a very unusual and striking species of barn owl, which only lives on two Caribbean islands. This owl has a typical barn owl 'look' but its rich reddish body colour and smoky grey face set it apart. Although the Ashy-faced Owl shares its island homes with the closely related American Barn Owl, the two species do not seem to interact with each other.

Features

Ashy-faced Owls are a rather startling, bright gingery-red colour, with dark grey mottling on their wings. The underside has delicate, darker barring. They have a heart-shaped face, outlined with a thick orange border, which is a rich, almost blueish shade of grey. The small, black eyes have dark smudges at their inner edge, making them look larger.

Hunting

Little is known about this owl's way of life in the wild, as there are few ornithologists active in the countries where it lives. The diet is known to consist mainly of mice and rats, as well as insects, small birds and reptiles. The Ashy-faced Owl's hunting methods are probably similar to the other barn owl species.

Call & Song

The owl gives a drawn-out, harsh and rasping wheeze, which is likely to be its version of a territorial song, and it also makes soft clicking sounds.

Size

Male	33–34 cm (13–13½ in)
Female	34–35 cm (13½–13¾ in)
Wingspan	not known

Habitat & Distribution

The two islands in the Caribbean where the Ashy-faced Owl is found are Hispaniola (comprising Haiti and the Dominican Republic) and the tiny island of Tortuga. It lives in open countryside including farmland.

TAWNY OWL
STRIX ALUCO

The classic 'Brown Owl' of many British children's stories, the TAWNY OWL is a common woodland owl of western Europe. This owl is responsible for the familiar 'to-whit, to-whoo' call, which can be heard in parks and gardens as well as woodlands. The largest British owl, the Tawny Owl dominates other species and may drive them from its territory.

Features

A very round, fluffy-looking owl with short wings and tail, the Tawny Owl occurs in a red-brown and a grey colour morph, with intermediates between these two. The plumage pattern is a subtle and complex mix of fine barring, dark streaks and paler speckles. The owl's round face and big, dark eyes give it a gentle, almost timid look, which belies its assertive personality.

Hunting

Strictly nocturnal, the Tawny Owl hunts from a favourite perch and, with its superb hearing, can detect the smallest rustle from a moving animal on the ground below, whereupon it pounces onto its prey. The diet is mainly small mammals but also includes earthworms, fish and small birds.

Call & Song

The drawn-out, fluty 'hoo-hoo-whoooo' hoot is a familiar woodland call, given by both sexes as a territorial song. There is also a sharp 'kee-vick' call, which indicates alarm or aggression.

Size

Male ....36–41 cm (14¼–16¼ in)

Female ....40–46 cm (16–18 in)

Wingspan ....94–105 cm (37–41 in)

Habitat & Distribution

Tawny Owls occur in most of Europe (except Ireland and northern Scandinavia) and into western Asia. They live in woodlands of all kinds as well as more open areas with scattered trees.

BARN OWL
TYTO ALBA

Known by many folk names including 'white owl' and 'screech owl', the BARN OWL is a beautiful owl that lives mainly in open countryside and takes its name from its habit of nesting inside farm buildings. Barn Owls have one of the most extensive natural ranges of any wild bird, although in some countries they have become very rare, mainly because of changes to their habitat.

Features

There is some variation between the different subspecies, but most Barn Owls are very pale, with the face, breast, belly and the undersides of the wings all being white. The upper side is sandy yellow-brown, mottled with grey. Their eyes are small and black, and their legs and wings long. When seen in flight, the Barn Owl often looks pure white, hence its alternative British name 'white owl'.

Hunting

Barn Owls often hunt in flight, using the breeze to give them lift as they fly slowly just above the ground, sometimes hovering to look for prey. On windy nights or when the breeze is too light they prefer to hunt from a perch. They feed mainly on voles.

Call & Song

The territorial call is a long, harsh, chilling screech with a hissing quality. The young owls beg for food with a curious 'snoring' call.

Size

Male ....29–40 cm (11½–15¾ in)

Female ....33–44 cm (13–17¼ in)

Wingspan ....85–98 cm (33½–38½in)

Habitat & Distribution

This owl is very widespread, occurring across Europe and Africa, the Arabian peninsula and South-East Asia. It is an open-country and farmland bird but has declined in many areas. In Britain, though, favourable farming schemes and purpose-built nest boxes have reversed this trend.

DARK-BREASTED BARN OWL

TYTO ALBA GUTTATA

Barn Owls of central and eastern Europe belong to a distinct subspecies, which is sometimes called the DARK-BREASTED BARN OWL. These owls look quite different to the mostly white birds of Britain and western Europe, with their rich brown and dark grey plumage, although they are similar in their habits. Occasionally, a Dark-breasted Barn Owl will migrate west to Britain and join its pale-breasted cousins.

Features

Dark-breasted Barn Owls are similar in size and shape to the paler Barn Owls of Britain, but their plumage is several shades darker. The breast and belly is a rich red-brown, sprinkled with small, dark spots, and the wings are mainly dark grey mixed with red-brown and speckled with tiny, white dots. The face is almost pure white and contrasts strongly with the rest of the plumage.

Hunting

These owls use the same hunting methods and take the same kinds of prey as other barn owl subspecies. Because their hunting success is very strongly influenced by the weather, if they fail one night they may hunt the next day in broad daylight.

Call & Song

The typical quavering Barn Owl screech, this species' version of a territorial song, is given most often in late winter and early spring. When agitated, they hiss or snap their bills.

Size

Male ....29–40 cm (11½–13 in)

Female ....33–44 cm (13½–17¼ in)

Wingspan ....85–98 cm (33½–38½ in)

Habitat & Distribution

The Dark-breasted Barn Owl occurs in central and eastern Europe. At the western edge of its range it interbreeds with the much paler western European subspecies. It lives mainly in open countryside.

RUFOUS-LEGGED OWL

STRIX RUFIPES

A very shy and elusive owl, the RUFOUS-LEGGED OWL is found on mountain slopes in southern South America. This species belongs to the wood owl group and is a stocky, medium-sized owl with beautifully patterned plumage. It is thought to be a rather rare bird, although its strictly nocturnal way of life makes it difficult for researchers to study.

Features

Like the other wood owls, the Rufous-legged Owl is a thickset bird with a large, round head. The plumage on the back and wings is dark grey-brown, evenly scattered with large, pale spots. On the breast and belly there is bold, dark and light barring. The face is reddish-brown, with a prominent whitish 'moustache' around the bill, and the eyes are very dark brown. The legs and toes are covered in reddish-brown downy feathers.

Hunting

The Rufous-legged Owl hunts primarily from a perch, typically a tree branch, where it listens for sounds of movement. Its diet is quite varied, consisting of small mammals, lizards, small birds, insects and whatever other small creatures it encounters.

Call & Song

The males have a territorial song consisting of a series of quick throaty notes, given at high volume during the breeding season. The female's reply is similar but higher-pitched.

Size

Male	33–36 cm (13–14¼ in)
Female	35–38 cm (13¾–15 in)
Wingspan	not known

Habitat & Distribution

The Rufous-legged Owl is found in southern Chile and south-western Argentina, down to the southern tip of South America. This is a bird of forested mountain slopes, from sea level to 2,000 m (6,561 ft) at least.

BOOBOOK

NINOX NOVAESEELANDIAE

Australia has relatively few owl species. The commonest and best known is the Boobook or Southern Boobook, named for its two-note song. The Boobook is active only at night, although its daytime hiding place is sometimes given away if small birds find it – they will loudly mob it until it flies away. Boobooks live wherever there are trees, including in towns.

Features

The Boobook's plumage colour is very variable, but in all its forms it has a distinctive shape, with long wings and tail, and a rather small head. The facial disc is not clearly defined, making it look hawk-like rather than typically 'owlish'. The plumage is softly dappled grey or grey-brown and whitish all over, with some forms quite reddish on the breast. The rather bulging eyes are bright yellow, giving it an intensely startled expression.

Hunting

This owl takes a variety of small prey, including birds and mammals but particularly insects, which it may catch in flight. In towns, Boobooks are sometimes seen catching moths and beetles around street lights.

Call & Song

The Boobook gets its name from its territorial song, a repeated and clear two-note hoot. The song is sometimes preceded by softer croaks. Among its calls is a cat-like miaow.

Size

Male	25–32 cm (9¾–12½ in)
Female	28–36 cm (11–14¼ in)
Wingspan	188–261 cm (74–102¾ in)

Habitat & Distribution

The Boobook is quite widespread in Australia, apart from the interior deserts, and is also found in New Guinea and the Lesser Sunda islands. It can be found in woodland, parks and gardens.

BURROWING OWL
ATHENE CUNICULARIA

A very distinctive, small owl with comically long legs, the BURROWING OWL lives in North and South America. This owl is unusual in many ways – it nests in underground burrows, is relatively gregarious and is active in the daytime as well as at dusk. The owl's charm makes it very popular with the general public, but it is endangered in some areas.

Features

This owl has a slim, broad-headed outline, often standing very upright on its long legs. Its plumage is dark brown on the crown, back and wings, with white spots, and paler below with dark patches. It has broad white 'eyebrows', giving the appearance of frowning, and large, bright yellow eyes. Males are often sun-bleached, because they 'stand guard' outside the burrows.

Hunting

Burrowing Owls hunt by day and live mainly on invertebrates, preferring substantial beetles, scorpions and moths. They will also eat small mammals and lizards. The usual hunting method is to watch from a perch, but they will also chase prey on foot and can catch insects in flight.

Call & Song

This is a sociable bird and uses many calls. The male's song is a plaintive, three-note whistled hoot. In alarm, it gives a dry rattle.

Size

Male	19–23 cm (7½–9 in)
Female	20–25 cm (7¾–9¾ in)
Wingspan	not known

Habitat & Distribution

Although found from southern Canada down to southern Argentina, this owl's distribution is patchy. It lives in open country – grassland, semi-desert and farmland – but heavy insecticide use has caused it to decline severely in some areas.

WESTERN SCREECH OWL

MEGASCOPS KENNICOTTII

A small North American owl, the WESTERN SCREECH OWL sports pointed ear tufts. This is a nocturnal owl, which relies on its camouflage when it is hiding in its daytime roost, so may not fly away even if closely approached. In common with some other screech owls, it comes in different colour forms or 'morphs', some dull grey and others bright gingery brown.

Features

The Western Screech Owl is a small but sturdy owl, whose entire appearance changes considerably with its mood – when alert, its posture becomes tall and slim, its ear tufts stand erect and its bright yellow eyes narrow to a squinting glare. The plumage has a camouflaged pattern resembling tree bark, and may be grey, reddish or somewhere in between.

Hunting

This owl's diet is mainly composed of insects and other invertebrates, but also small birds and mammals, especially in winter when insects are more scarce. Occasionally, Western Screech Owls bring blind snakes to their nests which, if not eaten by the chicks, live in the nest and keep it free of parasites.

Call & Song

Both sexes have a main song consisting of two purring, trilling notes. A secondary song is an accelerating trill.

Size

Male	22–23 cm (8¾–9 in)
Female	23–24 cm (9–9½ in)
Wingspan	not known

Habitat & Distribution

This owl lives down the western side of North America, from south-western Canada to Mexico. It lives anywhere there are trees, from thick riverside forests to suburban gardens. Although quite common, it is declining because of forest clearance in some areas.

TROPICAL SCREECH OWL
MEGASCOPS CHOLIBA

There are many kinds of screech owl in South America and most of them are rare, but the TROPICAL SCREECH OWL is both very widespread and fairly common, mainly because it lives in many different kinds of habitats. Active at night, it hunts insects from dusk until dawn, and in the breeding season males will give their sweet, trilling song for hours at a time.

Features

A solidly built small owl, the Tropical Screech Owl varies considerably in colour, with grey, brown and reddish morphs. It has yellow eyes and rather small ear tufts, which are completely flattened when it is relaxed. The facial disc has a strong dark border and the chest is pale with dark streaks. The owl's back has pale stripes or 'shoulder braces', which help with camouflage by breaking up its pattern.

Hunting

Like most screech owls, it is mainly an insect-eater, liking fat moths and large, meaty beetles. Small reptiles, mammals and birds supplement its diet. Watching from a perch, the owl jumps down to grab its prey, and sometimes chases insects in flight.

Call & Song

The main song for both sexes is a trill followed by some short, clear, fluty notes. Their alarm call, strangely, sounds rather like laughter.

Size

Male ....20–23 cm (7¾–9 in)

Female ....22–25 cm (8¾–9¾ in)

Wingspan ....not known

Habitat & Distribution

This owl has an extensive range, from Central America down through most of South America except the Andes and the far south. It avoids the thickest tropical forest, preferring more open woodland types, where it can be quite common.

GREAT HORNED OWL

BUBO VIRGINIANUS

Apart from the Snowy Owl, the GREAT HORNED OWL is the only one of the eagle owls found in North America. This is a big and powerful owl, which varies in colour across its range. Birds in colder climates are larger and paler than those in the tropics. Great Horned Owls will live in suburban areas, as well as wild countryside.

Features

Although Great Horned Owls can vary in plumage colours and size, they are usually easy to recognize because there are no other very big owls with ear tufts in most of their range. This owl is a hefty, solid bird with an imposing, orange-eyed glare and large, cat-like ear tufts. The plumage is strongly patterned with dark mottling, streaks and barring on a paler background. When the owl is calling, its pure white throat feathers are puffed out and become very noticeable.

Hunting

These owls are powerful hunters, mainly catching medium-sized mammals — even pet cats and dogs. Their diet also includes birds, reptiles, amphibians and insects. They usually hunt from a perch, but sometimes also in flight.

Call & Song

This big owl has a big voice, the male giving a territorial song consisting of a series of five deep, booming hoots. The female's reply is similar.

Size

Male ....45–58 cm (17¾–22¾ in)

Female ....50–64 cm (19¾–25¼ in)

Wingspan ....91–152 cm (35¾–59¾ in)

Habitat & Distribution

This owl is found across North America (excluding the far north) and down into north-western South America. A separate population lives in south-eastern South America. It lives in all kinds of woodland, except thick rainforest.

SPECTACLED OWL
PULSATRIX PERSPICILLATA

The SPECTACLED OWL takes its name from the pale markings on its otherwise dark face, which give this large and handsome owl a very distinctive appearance. Spectacled Owls live in dense rainforests, following a secretive nocturnal lifestyle that has been little studied. Deforestation is a potentially serious threat to the survival of this species.

Features

A gorgeous-looking owl, the Spectacled Owl has a colour scheme of chocolate brown above and warm cream below, in blocks of solid colour that lack the speckling, streaking and barring seen on most owls. The pale spectacle markings frame large, yellow-orange eyes, and give an intense expression. As a hot-climate bird, it looks sleeker and less fluffy than more northern owls, but still has a rounded and large-headed outline.

Hunting

All kinds of small animals are potential prey for Spectacled Owls, from mice and birds to crabs and spiders. The owl usually hunts from a favourite branch, pouncing on prey it spots on the ground or on a lower branch.

Call & Song

The song, given by both sexes, is a series of dry, hollow calls that sound more like the taps of a woodpecker than an owl's hoots. The species is called the 'knocking owl' in Brazil.

Size

Male	43–48 cm (17–19 in)
Female	46–52 cm (18–20½ in)
Wingspan	not known

Habitat & Distribution

Spectacled Owls live in South America, except the far west and south, and extend north through Central America into southern Mexico. They like all kinds of woodland but especially rainforest. Although at risk from logging activities reducing their habitat, their numbers are not yet declining significantly.

URAL OWL

STRIX URALENSIS

The Ural Owl is a notoriously fierce bird – the Swedish call it the 'strike owl' for its habit of attacking anyone who dares go near its nest. This is a large, pale grey, round-headed owl, found mainly in pine forests across north-eastern Europe and Asia. In some areas, conservationists supply nest boxes for Ural Owls, leading to a significant increase in their population.

Features

This owl looks both large and long when perched, with a big head and long wings and tail giving it an attenuated rear end. The soft grey plumage is streaked dark on the underside and marbled with paler tones on the back and wings, giving it a frosted appearance. The Ural Owl looks rather like a super-sized Tawny Owl, its black eyes giving it the same mild expression.

Hunting

Most of the Ural Owl's prey is voles, but it is big and strong enough to catch much larger prey and sometimes takes birds up to the size of grouse, and mammals as large as young hares. This owl hunts by watching from a high perch.

Call & Song

The male's song is a series of 10 to 12 rather soft, low, fluty hoots. The female's version is more rasping and higher-pitched.

Size

Male .... 50–56 cm (19¾–22 in)

Female .... 54–62 cm (21¼–24½ in)

Wingspan ..... 115–135 cm (45¼–53¼ in)

Habitat & Distribution

Ural Owls are found across north-eastern Europe and into Asia, including Japan. There are also separate populations in southern Europe. This is an owl of pine forests and damp mixed woodland, and it is quite a common bird.

VERMICULATED EAGLE OWL
BUBO CINERASCENS

A relatively small eagle owl, the VERMICULATED EAGLE OWL used to be considered a form of the Spotted Eagle Owl but is now regarded as a species in its own right. This owl has rather flat ear tufts that stick out at the sides. A bird of open country, it is more likely to nest and roost among rocks and crags than in trees.

Features

A beautiful owl with soft dove-grey plumage, the Vermiculated Eagle Owl is sometimes known as the 'Greyish Eagle Owl'. The word 'vermiculated' comes from the Latin word for 'worm' and refers to the fine, wavy, dark barring or vermiculation on the bird's breast and belly. Like its larger cousin, Verreaux's Eagle Owl, it has big, black eyes, and blackish edges to its facial disc.

Hunting

These nocturnal owls are known to catch large flying insects and also bats on the wing, but they also eat ground-dwelling animals such as rodents, lizards and large spiders, which they catch by dropping on them from a perch. Further study is needed to determine the make-up of this owl's diet more accurately.

Call & Song

This owl gives a song consisting of a low double hoot, the first note more abrupt and the second softer, longer and deeper.

Size

Male	43 cm (17 in)
Female	43 cm (17 in)
Wingspan	not known

Habitat & Distribution

The Vermiculated Eagle Owl is found in a band across central Africa, from Senegal and Cameroon across to northern and central Kenya. Here it lives in light woodland, savannah, semi-desert and suburban areas. It has not been studied a great deal but is not considered to be a common species.

INDIAN SCOPS OWL

OTUS BAKKAMOENA

The scops owls make up the biggest group of owl species in the world. The INDIAN SCOPS OWL is a fairly typical example of the group – a small, rather slim owl with large and very prominent, pointed ear tufts. There are several subspecies of this owl, with those living in the north being much paler than the southern forms.

Features

The Indian Scops is a pale, short-bodied and very petite owl, with a light grey-brown back and wings, and a creamy belly with fine, dark streaks. Its ear tufts are shaped and positioned very much like a cat's ears, and have dark outer edges which look like shadows, making the tufts appear more three-dimensional. The large eyes are dark brown, and often held half-closed in a squint.

Hunting

Like other scops owls, this species is mainly insectivorous; larger kinds such as crickets, grasshoppers and beetles are preferred. It will sometimes take small mammals and lizards. Although it usually hunts from a perch, it will catch moths in flight and may loiter around street lamps to catch insects.

Call & Song

Singing birds give a rather croaking single note at regular intervals, and may keep this up for hours. It also has a chattering call, although the function is unknown.

Size

Male	20–21 cm (7¾–8¼ in)
Female	21–22 cm (8¼–8¾ in)
Wingspan	61–66 cm (24–26 in)

Habitat & Distribution

This owl is common in India as well as southern Pakistan, Nepal and much of Sri Lanka. Requiring trees for nesting, it lives in woods, gardens and orchards.

SOUTHERN WHITE-FACED OWL

PTILOPSIS GRANTI

A small owl from the southern half of Africa, related to the scops owls, the SOUTHERN WHITE-FACED OWL is distinctive and beautiful, and familiar to many people as it is widely kept in zoos and aviaries. In the wild, it lives in scrubland, savannah and light forest, and at night it hunts all kinds of prey from insects up to squirrels.

Features

A very monochrome bird with striking bright red-orange eyes, the Southern White-faced Owl has plumage patterned in black, white and shades of grey. Its white face is thickly outlined with black, and its grey body has fine but clear black streaks, like pencil lines. When relaxed it looks round and plump, with flattened ear tufts, but when startled it becomes thinner, with narrowed eyes and upright tufts.

Hunting

All kinds of small creatures are eaten, from spiders and scorpions to small birds and mammals. This owl hunts by night, finding a well-hidden perch from where it listens and watches for movement, before gliding down to grab its prey, or moving to a closer perch.

Call & Song

This owl's territorial song begins with a trill and ends with an upward-inflected longer note. Both sexes sing, and also exchange various shorter notes with each other.

Size

Male	22–23 cm (8¾–9 in)
Female	23–24 cm (9–9½ in)
Wingspan	not known

Habitat & Distribution

This is quite a common bird in southern Africa, found south of Cameroon and Kenya, and in the northern part of South Africa. A bird of open savannah and thorny scrubland, it will also live around villages.

CAPE EAGLE OWL

BUBO CAPENSIS

The Cape Eagle Owl is so called because it can be found at the Cape in South Africa, although it also occurs further north-east on the continent. This is a big, dark-plumaged owl with very long ear tufts and a rather severe expression. The Cape Eagle Owl is a nocturnal species, which lives mainly in open landscapes but also visits towns, where it hunts pigeons.

Features

Large and solid, this is an imposing owl. The grey-brown plumage is very heavily patterned with dark splotches on both upper and under sides. The back bears whitish 'shoulder braces' and the throat and feet are also pale. The long, fine and blackish ear tufts surmount a broad face dominated by huge, heavy-lidded orange-yellow eyes.

Hunting

Like all eagle owls, this bird is a formidable hunter, and has been known to kill birds as large as the heron-like Hamerkop, which stands as tall as the Cape Eagle Owl itself. Its diet also includes mammals as large as hares, and a wide range of smaller mammals, along with lizards, snakes and frogs.

Call & Song

Males and females have a three-note song, the middle hoot being long and drawn-out compared to the first and last notes. The owl's alarm call is a barking note.

Size

Male	....	46–52 cm (18–20½ in)
Female	....	50–58 cm (19¾–22¾ in)
Wingspan	....	120–125 cm (47¼–49 in)

Habitat & Distribution

The Cape Eagle Owl's range covers South Africa and extends patchily up the eastern side of the continent to Ethiopia. It prefers rocky, open countryside, and its population is stable.

MAGELLAN HORNED OWL
BUBO MAGELLANICUS

Once considered to be a subspecies of the Great Horned Owl, the MAGELLAN HORNED OWL has been found to have different calls and songs to that species and so is now treated separately. A fairly big, stocky owl with ear tufts, it is found in South America; in Chile, it is called 'Tucúquere' after the rhythm of its song.

Features

This owl resembles the Great Horned Owl but is more lightweight, with weaker legs and feet. A rather squat-shaped bird, it is mainly grey in colour with fine, darker barring on its belly. A pair of dark 'eyebrows' leading up and outwards from the eye corners to the ear tufts, give it a frowning expression, which is accentuated by the bright yellow eyes and heavy upper eyelids.

Hunting

All kinds of small to medium-sized mammals, birds and reptiles are fair game for this owl, with rabbits and hares being particular favourites. Like other eagle owls, it usually hunts from a high perch with a commanding view, and glides low and silently over the ground to catch its prey.

Call & Song

The territorial song is a double hoot, the stress on the second note, and then a soft purring sound, which is almost inaudible to the human ear.

Size

Male	45 cm (17¾ in)
Female	45 cm (17¾ in)
Wingspan	not known

Habitat & Distribution

This owl is found at the southern tip and western edge of South America, as far north as central Peru. It favours rocky, sometimes mountainous landscapes. Its population size and conservation status is not yet well understood.

MEXICAN STRIPED OWL
ASIO CLAMATOR FORBESI

One of the group known as 'eared owls', the MEXICAN STRIPED OWL is a subspecies of the Striped Owl, which occurs in Central and South America. This is a rather small and slim owl with very long ear tufts and large dark eyes. A nocturnal bird, it hunts in flight over open country, and in the daytime several may gather together and roost in the same tree.

Features

A rather dainty-looking owl, the Mexican Striped Owl is the smallest and palest subspecies of the Striped Owl, and has a charming appearance with its very large, dark eyes set under delicate whitish eyebrows, in a pale face outlined with dark 'pencil lines'. The stripes that give it its name are the bold, dark streaks on its pale chest. The upper parts are reddish-brown with darker mottling.

Hunting

This owl is an expert aerial hunter, flying low over rough grassland or savannah and using both eyes and ears to detect mice and other potential prey moving below. Sometimes it will also hunt from a raised perch, such as a fence post.

Call & Song

The singing male gives a single, quite long hoot, then repeats it after several seconds. The hoot is relatively high-pitched with a rising inflection, giving it a question-like sound. The female's version is higher-pitched.

Size

Male ....30–32 cm (11¾–12½ in)

Female ....31–33 cm (12¼–13 in)

Wingspan .... not known

Habitat & Distribution

This owl is found from southern Mexico down through Costa Rica and Panama, and is geographically separated from the other subspecies of Striped Owl that are found in South America. It lives in grassland and along woodland edges.

GREAT GREY OWL

STRIX NEBULOSA

A large and beautiful owl of northern forests, the GREAT GREY OWL is instantly recognizable because of its huge-headed shape and unique face pattern of concentric circles. For its size, this owl is very lightweight; most of its bulk is formed by thick plumage that helps it endure the cold of Arctic regions. A Great Grey Owl played the Weasley family's hapless 'Errol' in the *Harry Potter* films.

Features

No other owl could be confused with the Great Grey Owl. A dappled grey bird, its shape is very top-heavy, the head looking especially huge when the bird is in its slim, alert posture, with its body plumage drawn in. The small, yellow eyes, looking deep-set within its broad face, give it a thoughtful expression. Under its bill it has a patch of black, like a neat beard.

Hunting

Great Grey Owls feed on various small animals but mainly voles, which they can catch even when the voles are under a crust of snow — the owls hear them moving and punch through the snow with bunched-up feet. They hunt both in flight and from perches.

Call & Song

This owl's territorial song is a series of short, evenly spaced deep hoots, with up to 12 notes over an eight-second spell.

Size

Male .... 57–65 cm (22½–25½ in)

Female .... 61–70 cm (24–27½ in)

Wingspan .... 130–160 cm (51¼–63 in)

Habitat & Distribution

These owls have a wide distribution across northern Europe, Asia, Canada and northern North America. They live in patchy pine and mixed forests. Their population declines in years where vole numbers are low, but they can quickly recover.

LITTLE OWL
ATHENE NOCTUA

The LITTLE OWL is a compact, fierce-faced and long-legged bird. The species was introduced to England in the 19th century, by naturalists who knew Little Owls from Europe and wanted to see them locally. It also spread to Scotland and Wales. This is the species that is closely associated with the Greek goddess of wisdom, Athene.

Features

This owl's comically furious facial expression, coupled with its diminutive size, make it a very appealing little bird. This is further enhanced by its habit of vigorously bobbing its wide, rather flat-topped head when inspecting something of interest. Little Owls of more southern regions are pale sandy-coloured, but northern birds are darker and more grey, with lots of white speckling over the plumage, and all have bright yellow eyes under heavy white eyebrows.

Hunting

Little Owls eat mainly insects, which they catch by pouncing or swooping down from a perch, or sometimes by actively pursuing on foot. They also feed on earthworms and sometimes will eat small birds and mammals.

Call & Song

This owl's territorial song is a single hoot repeated every two seconds or so. The hoot is high-pitched, and when the bird is particularly excited it develops an explosive, yelping quality.

Size

Male ....21–22 cm (8¼–8¾ in)

Female ....22–23 cm (8¾–9 in)

Wingspan ....53–59 cm (20¾–23¼ in)

Habitat & Distribution

This species has a wide distribution in central Asia, northern Africa and Europe, including southern Britain. It has also been introduced into New Zealand. The Little Owl lives in open countryside.

BARRED OWL

STRIX VARIA

One of the more common of the North American owls, the BARRED OWL is a fairly large woodland owl. Although this species is nocturnal, it isn't shy and may fiercely attack people if they go too near its nest. Being a skilled and versatile predator, the Barred Owl has a very varied diet, sometimes even catching fish as well as baby alligators.

Features

A rather pale and bulky-looking owl, the Barred Owl has a barred pattern of white and light brown on its head, face and breast, and when its wings and tail are spread they also show a barred pattern. It has dark eyes and a bright yellow bill. The female is a little darker than the male, although this is only noticeable when a pair is together.

Hunting

Barred Owls will tackle all kinds of prey, although their main food is small mammals such as mice and voles. They usually hunt from a perch, but show inventiveness when it comes to attacking less conventional prey – for example, they have been observed wading in shallow water to catch fish.

Call & Song

The Barred Owl's song consists of several hooted notes, the rhythm of which is sometimes expressed as the phrase 'you cook today, I cook tomorrow'.

Size

Male .... 48–52 cm (19–20½ in)

Female .... 50–55 cm (19¾–21¾ in)

Wingspan ..... 107–111 cm (42½–43¾ in)

Habitat & Distribution

This North American owl is found mainly in the north and east of the continent. As it will nest in patchy forest, logging in the central states has allowed it to increase in numbers and spread westwards.

TURKMENIAN EAGLE OWL
BUBO BUBO TURCOMANUS

The Turkmenian Eagle Owl is one of several subspecies of the Eurasian Eagle Owl. This is one of the larger and lighter-coloured forms; its pale, dusty colouring helps it to blend in with the open, stony landscape that it inhabits in central Asia. Its distribution overlaps with that of the Indian Eagle Owl, and the two will readily interbreed.

Features

This light-coloured subspecies, with yellowish tones to its plumage, is perfectly disguised for its desert home. A large bird, it has powerful talons and bill. The large, bright orange eyes stand out dramatically against the soft, pale, greyish-yellow colours of its face. On the rest of the body, the pale background colour is quite boldly marked with darker streaks and barring.

Hunting

As with all Eurasian Eagle Owls, this bird is a force to be reckoned with, and feeds primarily on medium-sized birds and mammals. Rabbits and similar-sized mammals are its favourite fare. The owl may hunt from a perch, or, more rarely, it will take a low exploratory flight.

Call & Song

The territorial song is a two-note hoot, as with the other subspecies of Eurasian Eagle Owl. Other sounds include aggressive bill-snapping when threatened, and screaming begging calls from the chicks.

Size

Male .... 61–68 cm (24–26¾ in)

Female .... 65–75 cm (25½–29½ in)

Wingspan .... 150–180 cm (59–70¾ in)

Habitat & Distribution

This subspecies of Eurasian Eagle Owl is found in central Asia, from the Volga across to Mongolia. The owl is most likely to be encountered in open, rocky and semi-desert areas.

AFRICAN WOOD OWL

STRIX WOODFORDII

The African Wood Owl is a fairly small and rotund owl that lives in all kinds of woodland across most of sub-Saharan Africa. It is one of the more common and familiar African owls, although people are more likely to hear its hooting call at night than to see it because it is strictly nocturnal. The Zulu description of the call is 'Weh, mameh', meaning 'Oh, my mother!'.

Features

Compared to a typical robust wood owl such as the Tawny Owl, the African Wood Owl is quite a dainty-looking bird, although it still has the rotund shape typical of the group. Its plumage is delicately barred and mottled in shades of brown, grey and cream. The facial disc is only faintly defined, and the face is dominated by its large, gentle-looking, dark eyes. By day, it can be very approachable, standing its ground when spotted.

Hunting

African Wood Owls take a range of small animals, primarily insects and spiders but also lizards, mice and the odd small bird. They may hunt from a perch, or deftly swipe insects from tree leaves as they fly.

Call & Song

The male and female both have a song that consists of several loud, clear hoots in a rhythmic sequence, the male's being lower-pitched. The chicks beg for food with a high-pitched wheezing note.

Size

Male	30–33 cm (11¾–13 in)
Female	32–35 cm (12½–13¾ in)
Wingspan	79–80 cm (31–31½ in)

Habitat & Distribution

This owl is a fairly common bird across most of sub-Saharan Africa (aside from deserts) anywhere where there are trees, from ancient forest to town parks.

BLACK BARN OWL

TYTO ALBA — MELANISTIC FORM

Occasionally, a bird with a genetic mutation giving abnormal plumage is born. In the case of this 'BLACK BARN OWL', that abnormality is melanism – an excessive amount of the dark pigment melanin in the feathers. Birds with abnormal colours do not usually survive in the wild, as they stand out and don't have good camouflage, but this Barn Owl was born in captivity.

Features

The extra dark pigment in its plumage has given this Barn Owl a unique appearance. Although it belongs to the white subspecies *Tyto alba*, which normally has a white face and light sandy and grey wings, it is much darker than even the darkest subspecies. Melanism is very rare in wild birds. Rather more common is the reverse condition – leucism, where pigment is missing, resulting in a partly or entirely white bird.

Hunting

Owls with pigmentation abnormalities are likely to hunt just as successfully as their normal-coloured cousins, as long as they are nocturnal species. Their main problem comes by day when they are relying on their camouflage to roost safely.

Call & Song

Wild Barn Owls proclaim their territories with a harsh screech. An owl with melanism or leucism will be identical to the rest of its species in its calls.

Size

Male	29–35 cm	(11½–13¾ in)
Female	35–44 cm	(13¾–17¼ in)
Wingspan	85–98 cm	(33½–38½ in)

Habitat & Distribution

Barn Owls are found throughout most of Europe, Africa and South-East Asia; however, the chances of seeing a differently coloured species in the wild are very small.

STRIPED OWL
ASIO CLAMATOR

The Striped Owl is a South American cousin of the Long-eared Owl, sharing its distinctive, cat-like face and very prominent, erect ear tufts. Like other species of the genus *Asio*, this is a strikingly long-winged owl, with a very graceful, agile flight style. In common with the Long-eared Owl, it is relatively sociable and may roost and feed with others of its own kind.

Features

The Striped Owl is a fairly small and rather slimline owl. The ear tufts are long, fluffy-looking and positioned closer together than in any of the eagle owls. The Striped Owl is boldly patterned, with dark stripes down its front and dark barring on its wings, on a background of light reddish-brown. Its large eyes are dark.

Hunting

Striped Owls mainly feed on insects like moths, crickets, grasshoppers and beetles, and also take mice and voles. They hunt both in flight and from low perches, sometimes beginning their evening hunt at sunset but more usually not until after dark. On occasion, several Striped Owls may be seen hunting over one field if there is a particularly high abundance of voles.

Call & Song

The territorial song is a series of rather high, nasal hooting calls. This owl also has a harsh, barking alarm call, and begging chicks give a squeaky, downward-inflected screech.

Size

Male	30–34 cm (11¾–13½ in)
Female	33–38 cm (13–15 in)
Wingspan	not known

Habitat & Distribution

The Striped Owl's distribution runs from southern Mexico through Central America and parts of South America down to Uruguay. A common bird of open countryside, it lives in woodland edges and grasslands.

LONG-EARED OWL

ASIO OTUS

One of the world's more widespread owls, the LONG-EARED OWL is found across Europe, Asia and North America, and is a bird of light forest and woodland edges. It is very lightweight for its size, and is often chased and even killed by bigger, stronger owl species. It is rare in Great Britain but in Ireland, where there are no Tawny Owls, it is much more common.

Features

The Long-eared Owl often looks very tall and slim although it adopts a 'puffed-up' posture when threatened. Its plumage is beautifully patterned in shades of reddish-brown and grey, with darker markings. The ear tufts are long, closely spaced and upright. In flight, it looks very long-winged, and the wings are pale underneath with a black 'comma' mark at the wrist joint. Long-eared Owls in Eurasia have orange eyes, but the North American subspecies have yellow eyes.

Hunting

This owl hunts mainly small rodents, but takes more small birds in winter. Sometimes it hunts in flight, but if the weather is not conducive to this it will watch for prey from a perch instead.

Call & Song

Singing males give a single, deep, whooshing hoot at well-spaced intervals. The female's reply is weaker, with a squeaky 'toy trumpet' quality.

Size

Male ....35–38 cm (13¾–15 in)

Female ....36–40 cm (14¼–15¾ in)

Wingspan ....90–100 cm (35½–39¼ in)

Habitat & Distribution

A very widespread species, the Long-eared Owl occurs across most of Europe, the northern tip of Africa, across Asia via Japan to most of North America. Mainly found in woodlands, it also needs open country nearby for hunting.

BROWN WOOD OWL
STRIX LEPTOGRAMMICA

The Brown Wood Owl is a little-known forest bird of South-East Asia, including many of the Indonesian islands. Large, with distinctive rich red-brown colours, it is active only at night and if disturbed at its daytime roost, it will quickly and silently fly off among the trees. Although it is shy, it has a wide repertoire of songs and calls, given after sunset.

Features

The Brown Wood Owl is a rather dark bird, with a thickset, stocky outline. The face and upper chest are deep reddish-brown, but its belly is paler, marked with dark barring. The dark colour of the face means that the owl's eyes, which are also dark, are rather lost against their background, so unlike many owls it lacks a distinct facial expression.

Hunting

This owl, like most wood owls, feeds primarily on small mammals, especially rodents, but is not averse to trying other prey, and has been reported to take fish as well as small birds and insects. Usually it hunts from a favourite branch, from where it drops down when it hears prey moving below.

Call & Song

The Brown Wood Owl's song has two linked phrases – a short, initial hoot followed by a much more drawn-out and quavering note. Various alarm calls include barking and growling sounds.

Size

Male .... 34–40 cm (13½–15¾ in)

Female .... 40–45 cm (15¾–17¾ in)

Wingspan .... not known

Habitat & Distribution

The Brown Wood Owl is found in parts of India, Sri Lanka and down the Malay Peninsula to Borneo. A bird of dense tropical forest, its numbers are declining, mainly due to logging activity.

NORTHERN WHITE-FACED OWL

PTILOPSIS LEUCOTIS

The Northern White-Faced Owl is very similar to the Southern White-faced Owl, but scientists realized the two were different species when studies showed they have very different songs. Both are remarkably expressive birds, and their face shape can change dramatically according to their mood. The Northern White-faced Owl is also a popular bird in captivity.

Features

The Northern White-faced Owl looks almost exactly the same as the Southern White-faced – a small, smoky grey owl with vivid reddish eyes and long ear tufts. In general the Northern is a little larger and paler than the Southern, with a warmer tone to its grey plumage. Before it was known they are different species, they were allowed to cross-breed in captivity, so hybrids exist.

Hunting

This owl eats all kinds of small creatures including rodents, beetles, crickets and moths. It usually hunts from a perch, but can also chase insects in flight. It takes more small mammals than the closely related Scops Owls which are more insectivorous.

Call & Song

The song is simple, consisting of two fluty notes, the first very short, the second longer. The clear difference between the two white-faced owls' songs is why they are considered two separate species.

Size

Male	24 cm (9½ in)
Female	25 cm (9¾ in)
Wingspan	50cm (19¾ in)

Habitat & Distribution

This African owl is found from Senegal across to northern Kenya, with very little overlap with the Southern White-faced Owl's distribution. It is an owl of savannah and scrubland.

REPORTAGE

A gathering of friendly birds of *fine feather* waits in the wings. Turn the page for some quality face time with a *parliament of owls* photographed at close quarters. Now comes the hands-on part of the owl experience. No larking about and no ruffling of feathers. And no need for binoculars. It's EAGLE-EYED OWL TIME.

Screech Owl Sanctuary Cornwall, UK

We're on a wing and a prayer today.

I don't give a hoot!

Who-hoo are you looking at?

I am in cahoots with him.

OK, let's wing it!

Who-hoo's the best looking guy around here?

a flying masterclass.
Watch and learn:
it's all in the take-off.

I prefer to take it slowly...

Who-
cooks-
for-
you?

Coming in to land...

That's how it's done,
not a feather out of place.

We like the facilities around here. They wait on us hand and glove...

...and there's always a chance of a shoulder to fly from.

Rutland Falconry and Owl Centre Rutland, UK

always keep both eyes peeled!

an interloper! We're eagle-eyed, not eagle-friendly.

I've got my binocular vision with me.

Is this my best side? I can swivel my head up to 270 degrees if not...

Larking about outdoors during the day is owltastic. We should do it more!

Okay, here we go!

We turn heads (almost completely) wherever we go!

This is owl cool!

I can do this owl by myself, you know!

Hoots Owls
Leicestershire,
UK

We see a lot, we
hear a lot and
we know a lot...

...and a few treats.

...but sometimes it's nice to
have a helping hand

Chrissie's
Owls
Oxfordshire,
UK

Hmmm, looks like owl be seeing you again.

Feeling good today.
Let's wing it!

the
Gallery

GLOSSARY

Call any sound a bird makes that is not its song – includes sounds given when alarmed and when begging for food

Camouflage physical features, including colour and shape, that help an owl blend in with its habitat so it is less easily seen

Crepuscular active at dusk and dawn, sleeping at other times

Diurnal active by day, sleeping at night

Ear tufts pointed tufts of feathers on top of an owl's head, probably with a camouflage function (they are not related to actual ears)

Facial disc the flattened, round face of an owl, bordered by a 'ruff' of stiff feathers

Flight feathers the long feathers on the trailing edge of a bird's wing, which provide the power and lift for flight

Habitat the type of landscape that an animal lives in – for most owls, the habitat is woodland

Hover to be airborne on the spot, usually achieved by facing into the breeze and beating the wings rapidly

Hybrid an animal that is the result of a mating between two different species. Only very closely related species can produce hybrids, and hybrids are usually infertile or have reduced fertility

Invertebrate an animal without a backbone – includes insects, spiders, worms, crabs and snails

Migration a regular twice-yearly journey – typically south in autumn and back north in spring – made by an owl to avoid severe winter weather

Morph a distinct colour form of an owl – in several species, there are two or three colour morphs, often grey, red and brown

Nest box a man-made box with an entrance hole, designed and positioned so that wild birds will use it to nest inside

Nocturnal active at night, sleeping by day

Nomadic unlike migration, nomadic wandering may happen in any direction and at any time of year, usually as a response to changes in prey availability

Pellet a compacted mass of hair, bones and other indigestible parts of food, which an owl regurgitates some time after eating

Plumage the entire set of feathers on a bird

Predator any animal that catches and kills other animals for its food

Prey (noun) the living animals that an owl or other predator catches for its food; (verb) to hunt and catch living animals for food

Retina the part of the eye that absorbs light of various colours

Rodent small or medium-sized mammals with gnawing teeth, including mice, voles, rats, squirrels and lemmings

Savannah an environment of open grasslands with scattered trees and bushes

Song a particular sound or sequence of sounds that a bird makes when defending its territory or trying to attract a mate

Species a population of animals of the same 'type', which look the same and interbreed with each other

Subspecies some species can be further divided into distinct subgroups, but these groups will still interbreed, and are not distinct enough from each other to be considered different species, so they are classed as subspecies

Talons the claws of an owl or other bird of prey

Territory an area of land that a bird lives in and defends from others of the same species and sex

Vertebrate an animal with a backbone – mammals, birds, reptiles, amphibians and fish

OWL SANCTUARIES

ENGLAND

The Hawk Conservancy Trust:
Visitor Centre, Sarson Lane, Weyhill, Andover, Hampshire SP11 8DY; tel: +44 (0) 1264 773850; web: www.hawk-conservancy.org

The Barn Owl Centre:
Netheridge Farm, Netheridge Close, Hempsted, Gloucester GL2 5LE; tel: +44 (0) 1452 383999; web: www.barnowl.co.uk

World Owl Trust:
Muncaster Castle, Ravenglass, Cumbria CA18 1RQ; tel: +44 (0) 01229 717393; web: www.owls.org

SCOTLAND

World of Wings:
Blairlinn Cottages, Easter Blairlinn Road, Luggiebank, Cumbernauld, North Lanarkshire G67 4AA; tel: +44 (0) 1236 722999; web: www.worldofwings.co.uk

Wings Over Mull:
Auchnacroish House, Torosay, Craignure, Isle of Mull PA65 6AY; tel: +44 (0) 1680 812594, web: www.wingsovermull.com

WALES

Welsh Hawking Centre:
Weycock Road, Barry, South Glamorgan CF62 3AA; tel: +44 (0) 1446 734687; web: www.barrywales.co.uk/hawkingcentre

IRELAND

Burren Bird of Prey Centre:
Aillwee Cave, Ballyvaughan, Co Clare; tel: +00 353 (0) 657 077036; web: www.birdofpreycentre.com

GERMANY

Adlerwarte Berlebeck:
Hangsteinstraße (Parkplatz), D-32760 Detmold; tel: +0049 5231/47171; web: www.detmold-adlerwarte.de

Greifvogelpark:
Am Engelbach 1, 54439 Saarburg; tel: +0049 6581/996094; web: www.greifvogelpark-saarburg.de

SPAIN

Brinzal Rehabilitation Centre:
Albergue Juvenil, Casa de Campo, Madrid, 28011 Spain; tel: +0034 914 794 565/670 933 240; web: www.brinzal.org

US

World Bird Sanctuary:
125 Bald Eagle Ridge Road, Valley Park, Missouri, MO 63088; tel: +001 (636) 225 4390 ext. 0; web: www.worldbirdsanctuary.org

Eagle Valley Raptor Center:
927 North 343rd St West, Cheney, Kansas, KS 67025; tel: +001 (316) 393 0710; web: www.eaglevalleyraptorcenter.org

Carolina Raptor Center:
6000 Sample Rd., Huntersville, North Carolina, NC 28078; tel: +001 (704) 875 6521; web: www.carolinaraptorcenter.org

The Center for Birds of Prey:
4872 Seewee Road, Awendaw, South Carolina, SC 29429; tel: +001 (843) 971 7474: web: www.thecenterforbirdsofprey.org

Wildlife Learning Center:
16027 Yarnell Street, Sylmar, California, CA 91342; tel: +001 (818) 362 8711; web: www.wildlifelearningcenter.com

MSU's Kellogg Bird Sanctuary:
12685 East C Avenue, Augusta, Michigan, MI 49012; tel: +001 (269) 671 2510 www.kbs.msu.edu/visit/birdsanctuary

CANADA

The Owl Foundation:
R.R. 1, Vineland Station, Ontario L0R 2E0; web: www.theowlfoundation.ca

Wild Bird Care Centre:
735 Moodie Drive, Nepean, Ontario K2H 7V2; tel: +001 (613) 828 2849; web: www.wildbirdcarecentre.org

Orphaned Wildlife Rehabilitation Society (O.W.L.):
3800–72nd Street, Delta, British Columbia V4K 3N2; tel: +001 (604) 946 3171; web: www.owlcanada.ca

AUSTRALIA

Featherdale Wildlife Park:
217–229 Kildare Road, Doonside, New South Wales, NSW 2767 (near Blacktown); tel: +0061 (02) 9622 1644; web: www.featherdale.com.au

Flying High Bird Sanctuary:
Cnr Bruce Highway & Old Creek Road, Apple Tree Creek, Queensland 4660; tel: +61 7 4126 3777; web: www.flyinghighbirdsanctuary.net.au

Healesville Sanctuary:
Badger Creek Road, Healesville, Victoria 3777; tel: +0061 (03) 5957 2800; web: www.zoo.org.au

SOUTH AFRICA

Owl Rescue Centre:
Ruimsig, Roodepoort, Gauteng, 1732 South Africa; tel: +0027 82 719 5463; web: www.owlrescue911.webs.com

Raptor Rescue South Africa:
Lion Park Road, Pietermaritzberg, KwaZulu-Natal, 3730 South Africa; tel: +0027 031 785 4382; web: www.africanraptor.co.za

World of Birds:
Wildlife Sanctuary, Valley Road, Houtbay 7806, Western Cape; tel : +0027 021 790 2730; web: www.worldofbirds.org.za

OWL & WILD BIRD CHARITIES

UK

The Barn Owl Trust:
Waterleat, Ashburton, Devon TQ13 7HU; tel: +44 (0) 1364 653026; web: www.barnowltrust.org.uk

Hawk and Owl Trust:
PO Box 400, Bishops Lydeard, Taunton TA4 3WH; tel: +44 (0) 844 984 2824; web: www.hawkandowl.org

RSPB (Royal Society for the Protection of Birds):
The Lodge, Potton Road, Sandy, Bedfordshire; tel: +44 (0) 1767 680551; web: www.rspb.org.uk

Wing and a Prayer:
30, Cromer Road, Stratton Strawless, Norwich, Norfolk NR10 5LU; web: www.wingandaprayerhaven.org.uk

GERMANY

Nature and Biodiversity Conservation Union (NABU):
Berlin headquarters, Charitéstraße. 3, D-10117 Berlin, Germany; tel: +0049 3028 49840; web: www.nabu.de

US

Audobon Society:
225 Varick St, 7th Floor, New York, NY 10014; tel: +001 (212) 979 3000; web: www.audobon.org

CANADA

Bird Studies Canada:
P.O. Box 160, 115 Front Street, Port Rowan, ON N0E 1M0; tel: +001 (888) 448 2473; web: www.bsc-eoc.org

AUSTRALIA

BirdLife Australia:
Suite 2-05, 60 Leicester Street, Carlton VIC 3053; tel: +0061 (03) 9347 0757; web: www.birdlife.org.au

REFERENCES

The Barn Owl by David Chandler (2011), New Holland, London

A Delight of Owls – African Owls Observed by Peter Steyn (2010), Jacana Media, Johannesburg

North American Owls by P. A. Johnsgard (2003), Smithsonian Books, Washington

Owls by Marianne Taylor (2012), Bloomsbury, London

Owls of the World (Helm Identification Guides) by Claus Konig, Freidhelm Weick, Jan-Hentrick Becking (2008), Christopher Helm, London

Owls of the World: A Photographic Guide (Helm Photographic Guides) by Heimo Mikkola (2012), Christopher Helm, London

AUTHOR'S ACKNOWLEDGEMENTS

I'd like to thank Jayne Ansell for giving me the opportunity to write this book and organising everything in the early stages, and Jacqui Sayers for seeing things through to completion. A special thank you to Nigel Redman for putting me in touch with the folks at Ivy Press in the first place.

The copy-editor, Judith Chamberlain-Webber, did a great job checking through the text, and Virginia Zeal created the lovely design. My thanks go to Andrew Perris, whose stunning photos of the owls do full justice to the birds' beauty and presence.

I must also thank the workers and volunteers at the various owl sanctuaries whose birds are pictured in these pages, for allowing access and time with the owls. I have nothing but admiration for their work in looking after and rehabilitating owls that have come into their care through accident, injury or neglect.

My friends, as ever, were wonderfully supportive throughout – a special shout-out to Michèle, who gave valuable feedback on parts of the text.

PUBLISHER'S ACKNOWLEDGEMENTS

The publisher would like to extend their sincere thanks to the sanctuaries and owners who allowed us to photograph their owls for this book.

Hoots Hollows
www.hootsowls.co.uk
Cape Eagle Owl; Dark-breasted Barn Owl; Indian Scops Owl; Magellan Horned Owl; Northern White-faced Owl; Southern White-faced Owl; Ural Owl; Vermiculated Eagle Owl.

Screech Owl Sanctuary
www.screechowlsanctuary.co.uk
American Barn Owl; Ashy-faced Owl; Barn Owl; Boobook; Burrowing Owl; Eurasian Eagle Owl; Great Horned Owl; Indian Eagle Owl; Mottled Owl; Rufous-legged Owl; Snowy Owl; Spectacled Owl; Spotted Eagle Owl; Tawny Owl; Tropical Screech Owl; Verreaux's Eagle Owl; Western Screech Owl; Western Siberian Eagle Owl.

Rutland Falconry and Owl Centre
www.rutland-falconry.com
Barred Owl; Great Grey Owl; Little Owl; Mexican Striped Owl; Turkmenian Eagle Owl.

Chrissie's Owls
www.chrissiesowls.com
African Wood Owl; Black Barn Owl; Brown Wood Owl; Long-eared Owl; Striped Owl.

Thanks also to Knockhatch Falconry Centre, East Sussex.

INDEX

A
African witchdoctors 8
African Wood Owl 82, **83**
American Barn Owl 34, **35**
ancient civilizations 8
Ashy-faced Owl 38, **39**
Athene 8, 76

B
balance 12
Barn Owl 11, 18, 42, **43**
barn owls 9, 10, 14, 18, 34, 38, 42,
    44, 84
Barred Owl 10, 18, 78, **79**
bay owls 10
Black Barn Owl 84, **85**
Blakiston's Fish Owl 11, 18
Boobook 10, 48, **49**
breeding 16, 18
Brown Wood Owl 90, **91**
Burrowing Owl 17, 50, **51**

C
calls 7, 10, 16
Cape Eagle Owl 68, **69**
Chauvet Cave, France 8
chicks 16
Chrissie's Owls **107**
Common Scops Owl 17, 18
conservation 18, 60

D
Dark-breasted Barn Owl 44, **45**
desert owls 17
digestion 11
dinosaurs 9

E
eagle owls 8, 10, 11, 22, 24, 26, 28, 30,
    32, 56, 62, 68, 80
ear tufts 10, 14
eared owls 10, 72
ears 12
eggs 16
Egyptian hieroglyphs 8
Elf Owl 17
Eurasian Eagle Owl 22, **23**, 80
European Eagle Owl 10, 11
evolution 9
eyes 7, 12

F
falconry 7, 8, 22, 30
feathers 12, 14
feeding 11
filoplumes 12
fish owls 11, 18
flight 11, 12, 14
Forest Owlet 18
fossils 9

G
Galapagos Islands 9
Great Grey Owl 10, 11, 17, 74, **75**
Great Horned Owl 10, 56, **57**
Greece 8, 76

H
habitat 17
habitat loss 18, 42, 58
Harry Potter books/films 28, 74
hawk owls 10, 17, 48
hearing 12
Hoots Owls **106**
hunting 7, 9, 11, 12, 17

I
Indian Eagle Owl 30, **31**, 80
Indian Scops Owl 64, **65**
Indonesian islands 9, 90

L
Little Owl 11, 76, **77**
Long-eared Owl 17, 86, 88, **89**

M
Madagascar 8
Magellan Horned Owl 70, **71**
melanism 84
Mexican Striped Owl 72, **73**
migration 17, 44
monogamy 7, 16
morphs 52
Mottled Owl 36, **37**

N
neck 12
nest boxes 18, 60
nests 16
    underground 17, 50
nightjars 9
Northern Hawk Owl 17
Northern White-faced Owl 92, **93**

P
pesticides 18
plumage 7, 10, 14, 17, 84
pygmy owls 10

R
Rome 8
Rufous-legged Owl 46, **47**
Rutland Falconry and Owl Centre
    102-105

S
sanctuaries 7, 8, **96-107**
scops owls 9, 10, 17, 18, 64
Screech Owl Sanctuary **96-101**
screech owls 10, 52, 54
senses 12
Short-eared Owl 9, 17
Siau Scops Owl 18
Snowy Owl 17, 28, **29**
Southern White-faced Owl 66, **67**, 92
species 9, 10
Spectacled Owl 58, **59**
Spotted Eagle Owl 32, **33**
Spotted Owl 18
Striped Owl 86, **87**
superstition 7, 8, 18, 32

T
Tawny Owl 10, 11, 17, 40, **41**, 88
territoriality 7, 16, 40
Tropical Screech Owl 54, **55**
Turkmenian Eagle Owl 80, **81**

U
Ural Owl 60, **61**

V
Vermiculated Eagle Owl 62, **63**
Verreaux's Eagle Owl 26, **27**

W
Western Screech Owl 52, **53**
Western Siberian Eagle Owl 24, **25**
wings 14
wood owls 10, 11, 40, 46, 74, 78, 82, 90